eggberts

count-down for expectant fathers

CARTOONS BY
LAF

EGGBERT'S DIARY

EGGBERT'S COUNT-DOWN FOR EXPECTANT FATHERS

A brand new edition
in the form of a diary

Printed with permission

Compiled by Judi Quelland

With gratitude to Susie Barker Lavenson,
Daughter of Percy Barker, the original publisher.

Original cartoons by LAF
Lester A. Friedman

Copyright © 2010

EGGBERT
IS
BACK!

This time he is advising the male parent-to-be on solving such perplexing problems as:

- What to do when she demands cucumber sandwiches at 3:00 A.M.

- How to fortify yourself for the long stay in the hospital waiting room (don't forget your copy of PLAYBOY!)

- What to expect if you insist on being on the scene during delivery

- How to handle your paternal privileges in the pre-dawn hours (like the two o'clock feeding)

Eggbert shows you how to cope with these and all the other snares that lie in wait for your unsuspecting feet along the booby-trapped road from Count-Down to Splash-Down.

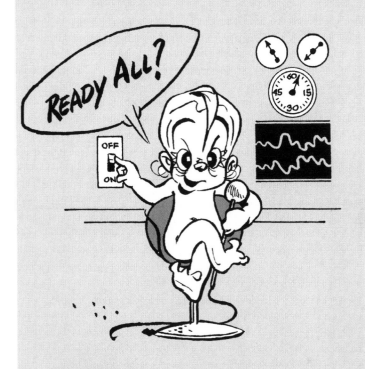

D (for "Delivery")

minus

9 (for "months")

D Minus 9·8·7...

WHAT DID YOU DO FIRST --
HIT THE BOTTLE OR KISS HER?

D Minus 9·8·7...

QUITE THE HE-MAN NOW, AREN'T YOU?

D Minus 9·8·7 . . .

AW, GO TO SLEEP ! IT WON'T
LOOK LIKE YOUR MOTHER-IN-LAW !

D Minus 9·8·7...

WELL ... WHO STARTED IT, ANYWAY ?

D Minus 9·8·7...

8 MONTHS TO GO AND SHE'S ALREADY
GOT YOU DOING THE HOUSEWORK ? ZEESH!

D Minus 9·8·7...

ALL OF A SUDDEN LIFE GOT DAMN
COMPLICATED, DIDN'T IT ?

D Minus 9·8·7 . . .

LOOKS LIKE YOUR NEST-EGG'S ALL GOING TO THE EGG, DOESN'T IT ?

D Minus 6·5·4...

SO WHAT IF IT'S 2 A.M.!
WHEN WE WANT A CUCUMBER
SANDWICH, WE <u>WANT</u> IT !

D Minus 6·5·4...

KICK US AGAIN IN YOUR SLEEP AND YOU'LL GET THE OTHER BARREL !

D Minus 6·5·4...

"TIC-TOC TIC-TOC" (THIS ORTA MAKE SOME MEDICAL JOURNAL !)

D Minus 6·5·4 . . .

SO, IS IT MY FAULT THE OLD MAN
BRINGS HER HOME TO ALASKA
TO SPAWN ?

D Minus 6·5·4...

... UP A LITTLE ... LITTLE MORE ...
WHOA ! SCRATCH RIGHT THERE, POP !

D Minus 6·5·4...

HE ALWAYS PUTS TOO MUCH LEMON
IN THE WHISKEY SOURS !

D Minus 6·5·4...

HE'S SURE TAKIN' ONE HELL OF
A LOT OF TRIPS, LATELY !

D Minus 6·5·4 . . .

LISTEN TO HIM ... TALKIN' ABOUT
HIS CAREFREE DAYS IN IRAQ !

D Minus 3·2·1...

WELL, I GUESS YOU GOTTA EXPECT
THINGS LIKE THIS IF YOUR
OLD MAN'S NAME IS MERLIN !

D Minus 3·2·1...

SO SHE'S TAKIN' UP TOO MUCH ROOM, EH ?
WANNA CHANGE PLACES, BUDDY ?

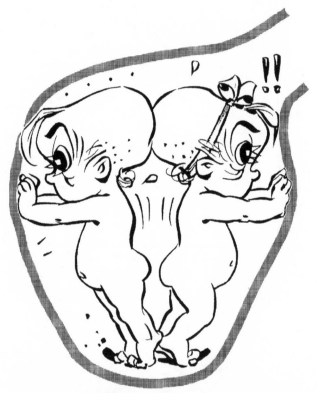

D Minus 3·2·1...

WA-HOO ! HAS SHE GOT POP BUFFALOED
WITH THAT "DELICATE CONDITION" GAG !

D Minus 3·2·1...

UH-UH! GETTIN' DOWN ON HIS
KNEES AIN'T GONNA SAVE POP ONE
NICKEL WITH <u>THIS</u> DOC!

D Minus 3·2·1...

WHO'S GONNA CUT <u>WHAT</u>
ON <u>WHOM</u> ?

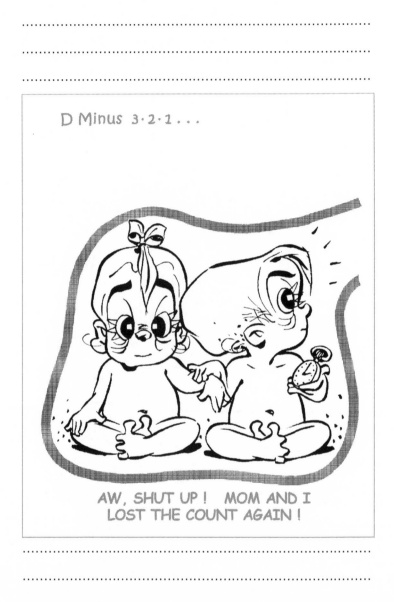

D Minus 3·2·1...

WE'RE ON OUR WAY. BUT I'LL
SWEAR, HE NEVER SLID
INTO HIS PANTS !

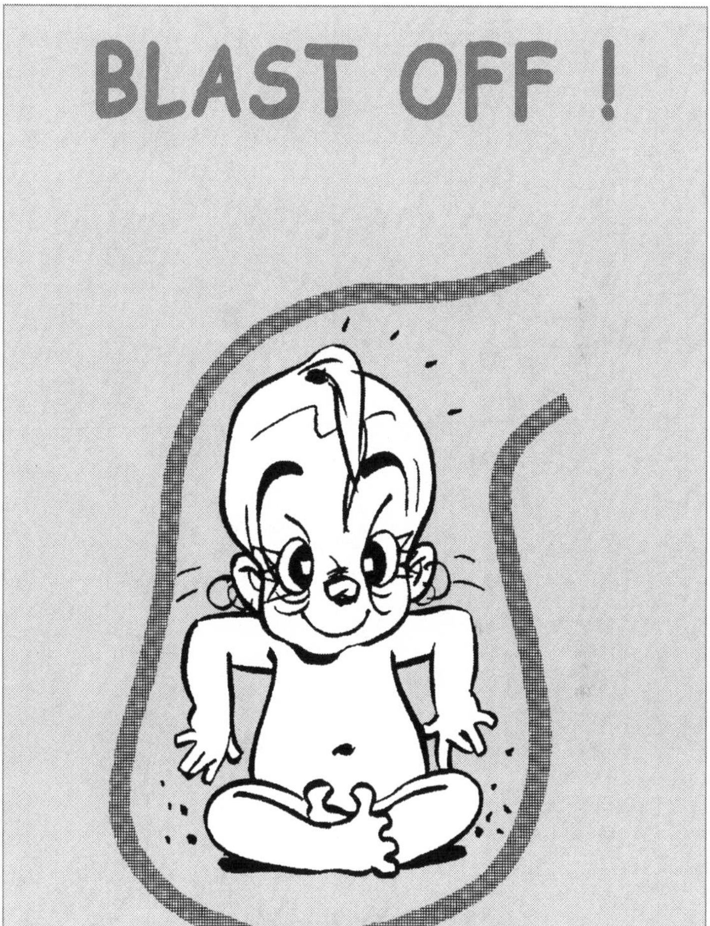
BLAST OFF !
. . . AND AWAY WE GO !

BLAST OFF !

WE'RE SWEATIN' IT OUT AND I'LL BET
HE'S ALREADY HALFWAY DOWN
TO THE BOWLING ALLEY !

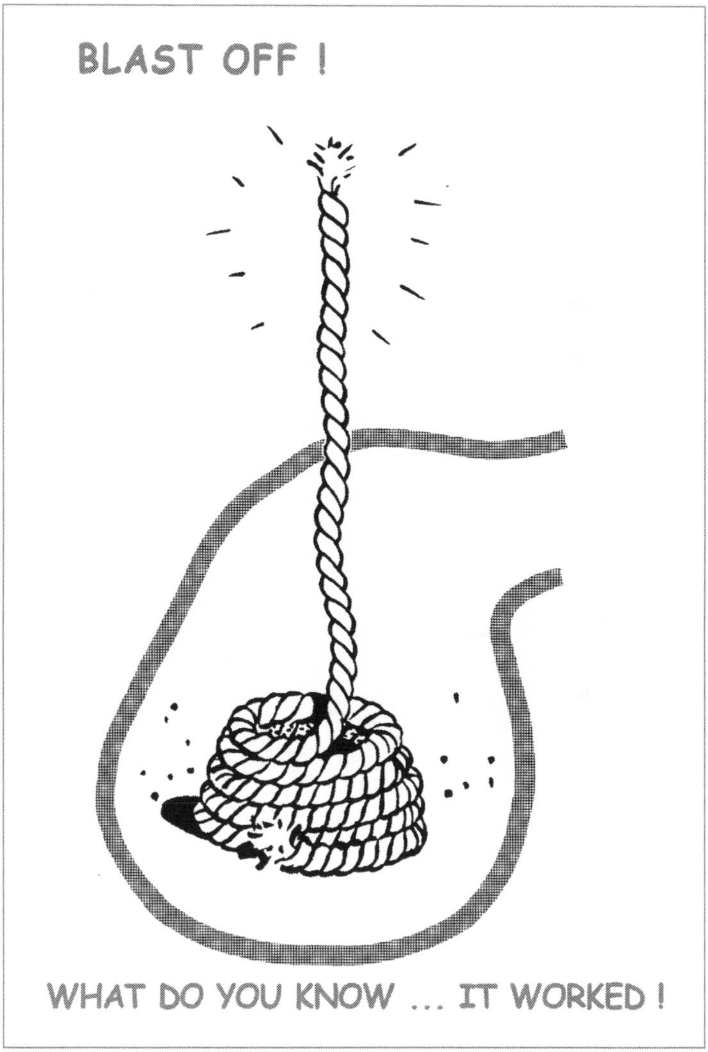
BLAST OFF !
WHAT DO YOU KNOW ... IT WORKED !

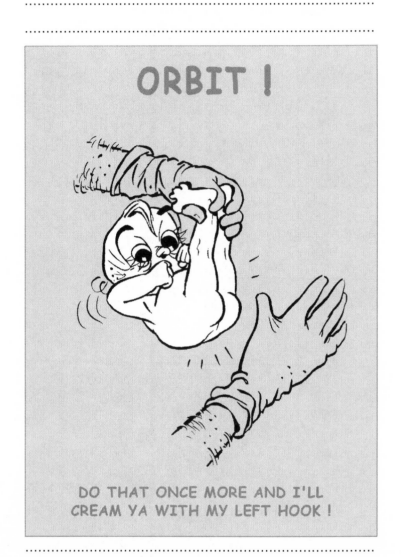

ORBIT !

SO... YOU INSISTED ON BEING IN THE DELIVERY ROOM, EH ? PULL YOURSELF TOGETHER AND THEY'LL RELEASE YOU FROM "INTENSIVE CARE" TOMORROW !

ORBIT !

NO, STUPID ... THEY PUT ON THE NAME BAND. HE WASN'T BORN WITH IT !

ORBIT !

HOW DO YA LIKE THAT, "BILLIARD-TOP" ?
YOUR KID WAS BORN WITH
MORE HAIR THAN YOU GOT !

ORBIT !

THINK AGAIN ... REAL HARD ! NOW,
WHY <u>AREN'T</u> WE BORN WITH TEETH ?

ORBIT !

LEAVE IT TO YOU, BIG HEART ! MOM'S
THE ONLY ONE IN THE WARD SEWING
BUTTONS ON YOUR SHIRTS !

SPLASH-DOWN !

GOWON ! HOLD THE KID . . .
YOU WON'T SQUASH IT !

SPLASH-DOWN !

UP AND AT EM', PAPA BIRD ! TIME TO
START SCRATCHIN' FOR WORMS !

SPLASH-DOWN !

COME ON, YOU'RE NOT SEASONING A HAMBURGER ! GIVE WITH THE <u>TALCUM</u> !

SPLASH-DOWN !

HE'S SNORING NICELY, NOW ... LET'S
GIVE HIM THE LATE, LATE SHOW !

SPLASH-DOWN !

KEEP YOUR SHAKY PAWS OFF ME !
THAT'S THE THIRD TIME YOU
DROPPED THE SOAP !

SPLASH-DOWN !

REMEMBER HOW CALM AND PEACEFUL
IT USTA BE AROUND THE HOUSE ?

SPLASH-DOWN !

WATCH IT, BUDDY ... OR WE'LL BE
OFF AND RUNNING AGAIN !